© 2024 by FAISAL JAMIL. All rights reserved.

Title: "The Art and Science of Customer Relationship Management"

This book, along with its contents encompassing text, illustrations, images, diagrams, and other creative elements, is the exclusive property of FAISAL JAMIL and is safeguarded by copyright law.

FAISAL JAMIL asserts full ownership and retains all rights to this book. No part of this publication may be reproduced, distributed, or transmitted in any form or by any means, such as photocopying, recording, or electronic methods, without prior written consent from the copyright holder. Brief quotations in critical reviews and certain noncommercial uses permitted by copyright law are exceptions.

This copyright notice applies to all editions, formats, and translations of the book, whether in print, digital, or any other medium or technology existing now or developed in the future. Unauthorized use or infringement may result in legal action and pursuit of remedies under applicable copyright laws.

While efforts have been made to ensure accuracy and reliability, FAISAL JAMIL does not guarantee the completeness or suitability of the information. Readers are responsible for evaluating and using the content judiciously.

FAISAL JAMIL reserves the right to make changes, updates, or corrections to the book without prior notice. Inclusion of third-party materials or references does not imply endorsement or affiliation unless used under fair use principles or with proper permissions and attributions.

For permissions, inquiries, or requests regarding the book's use, please contact FAISAL JAMIL through official channels listed on their Amazon author page or provided email address.

This comprehensive copyright notice serves to protect FAISAL JAMIL'S intellectual property rights, maintain content control, and inform users about associated restrictions and permissions.

Warm regards,

FAISAL JAMIL

For your feedback and reviews:

http://www.amazon.com/author/faisal.jamil

Email: faisaljamilauthor@gmail.com

About the author

Certainly! Faisal Jamil is a multifaceted individual with a diverse set of skills and experiences. With a strong foundation in computer knowledge since childhood, he has developed a deep understanding of technology that informs his work as a content writer. Faisal also possesses digital skills, which further enhance his abilities in various digital platforms and technologies.

Beyond his professional endeavors, Faisal Jamil has also excelled in the martial arts, particularly Shotokan Karate, where he achieved the prestigious rank of first Dan black belt. This achievement speaks to his dedication, discipline, and commitment to personal growth and mastery.

In his professional life, Faisal Jamil has carved out a successful career in sales management within the Fast Moving Consumer Goods (FMCG) sector. His roles in various FMCG companies have honed his skills in strategic planning, team leadership, and business development. Faisal's ability to drive sales and achieve targets has been instrumental in his career progression, showcasing his talent for identifying opportunities and delivering results.

Faisal Jamil is also deeply interested in business investment strategies, planning, and execution. His understanding of these areas has been key to his success in the business world, allowing him to make informed decisions and implement effective strategies. His ability to navigate the complexities of investment planning and execution has set him apart as a strategic thinker and a valuable asset in any business endeavor.

Overall, Faisal Jamil is a dynamic individual who combines his passion for technology, martial arts, sales management, digital skills, and business investment strategies to achieve success in diverse fields. His journey is a testament to his versatility, resilience, and continuous pursuit of excellence.

Yours Sincerely

FAISAL JAMIL

For your feedback and reviews:

https://www.amazon.com/author/faisal.jamil

Email: faisaljamilauthor@gmail.com

THE ART AND SCIENCE OF CUSTOMER RELATIONSHIP MANAGEMENT

Introduction

In today's competitive business landscape, maintaining strong and lasting relationships with customers is paramount. Customer Relationship Management (CRM) has evolved into a crucial strategy for businesses of all sizes to understand, engage with, and retain their customers. This book delves into the various facets of CRM, offering insights, strategies, and best practices for building and nurturing customer relationships that drive business growth and success.

Table of Content

Preface   8

Chapter 1: Understanding Customer Relationship Management   10

Chapter 2: Building a Customer-Centric Culture   17

Chapter 3: Data-Driven CRM Strategies   24

Chapter 4: Implementing CRM Systems   31

Chapter 5: CRM in Sales and Marketing   38

Chapter 6: CRM in Customer Service   48

Chapter 7: CRM Best Practices   51

Chapter 8: Future Trends in CRM   58

Conclusion   66

Preface

Welcome to "The Art and Science of Customer Relationship Management." In today's fast-paced and highly competitive business environment, building strong and lasting relationships with customers is more important than ever. Customer Relationship Management (CRM) is a strategic approach that helps businesses achieve this goal by focusing on understanding and meeting the needs of customers.

This book is designed to be a comprehensive guide to CRM, covering both the art and science behind effective customer relationship management. The art of CRM involves understanding customers' needs and preferences, building trust and loyalty, and delivering exceptional customer experiences. The science of CRM involves using data and analytics to personalize interactions, improve marketing and sales effectiveness, and drive business growth.

In this book, we will explore the evolution of CRM, the key components of CRM, and the importance of CRM in modern business. We will also discuss how to choose the right CRM system for your business, integrate it with existing systems, and train employees for effective CRM adoption. Additionally, we will explore how CRM can be used in sales and marketing, customer service, and other areas of the business.

We will also discuss best practices for CRM, including building long-term relationships, personalizing customer interactions, and balancing automation with human touch. Finally, we will explore future trends in CRM, such as the use of AI and machine learning, omni-channel customer engagement, and ethical considerations in CRM.

Whether you are new to CRM or looking to enhance your existing CRM strategies, this book will provide you with the knowledge and tools you need to succeed. Thank you for joining us on this journey into the world of Customer Relationship Management.

Chapter 1

Understanding Customer Relationship Management

A: Definition and Evolution of CRM

Customer Relationship Management (CRM) is a strategic approach that businesses use to manage and analyze interactions with current and potential customers. The goal of CRM is to improve customer retention, loyalty, and satisfaction by understanding their needs and preferences, analyzing data to personalize interactions, and using technology to streamline processes.

The evolution of CRM can be traced back to the early days of database marketing, where businesses used basic tools to manage customer information. As technology advanced, CRM systems became more sophisticated, allowing businesses to track and analyze customer interactions across multiple channels.

Initially, CRM was focused on automating sales and marketing processes, such as managing leads and tracking customer communications. However, businesses soon realized that CRM could be used for more than just automation. By analyzing customer data, businesses could gain insights into customer behavior and preferences, allowing them to personalize interactions and build stronger relationships.

Today, CRM is seen as a holistic approach to managing customer relationships. It involves not only technology but also strategies for customer engagement and relationship building. CRM systems are now more integrated with other business systems, such as marketing automation and customer service platforms, allowing for a more seamless customer experience.

Overall, CRM has evolved from a simple tool for automating sales and marketing processes to a comprehensive approach for managing customer relationships. By leveraging CRM effectively, businesses can improve customer satisfaction, increase loyalty, and drive business growth.

B: Importance of CRM in Modern Business

In today's highly competitive business environment, Customer Relationship Management (CRM) has become a critical strategy for businesses to differentiate themselves and build a loyal customer base. The importance of CRM in modern business can be seen in several key areas:

1: Improved Customer Relationships

CRM helps businesses better understand their customers' needs and preferences by consolidating customer information in a centralized database. This allows businesses to personalize their interactions with customers, providing better customer service and ultimately building stronger relationships.

2: Increased Sales and Revenue

CRM enables businesses to identify and target the most valuable customers, leading to increased sales and revenue. By analyzing customer data, businesses can identify upsell and cross-sell opportunities, as well as tailor marketing messages to specific customer segments.

3: Enhanced Customer Loyalty

By providing personalized experiences and anticipating customers' needs, CRM can help businesses build strong, long-lasting relationships with their customers. This can lead to increased customer loyalty and repeat business, as well as positive word-of-mouth referrals.

4: Better Marketing ROI

CRM allows businesses to track and analyze the effectiveness of their marketing campaigns. By measuring key metrics such as customer acquisition costs and customer lifetime value, businesses can optimize their marketing spend and improve ROI.

5: Improved Efficiency and Productivity

CRM streamlines and automates many customer-facing processes, such as lead management, sales forecasting, and customer support. This frees up employees to focus on more value-added tasks, improving efficiency and productivity.

Overall, CRM is a critical strategy for businesses looking to thrive in today's competitive business landscape. By leveraging CRM to improve customer relationships, increase sales and revenue, enhance customer loyalty, and improve efficiency, businesses can gain a competitive edge and drive business success.

C: Key Components of CRM

Customer Relationship Management (CRM) consists of several key components that work together to help businesses manage and improve their relationships with customers. These components can be broadly categorized into three main areas: people, processes, and technology.

1: People

People are at the heart of CRM. This includes both customers and employees. CRM focuses on building strong relationships with customers by understanding their needs and preferences, and providing personalized experiences. Empowering employees is also crucial, as they are the ones who interact with customers and deliver the customer experience. By empowering employees with the right tools and training, businesses can ensure that they are able to deliver exceptional customer experiences.

2: Processes

CRM involves defining and implementing processes for managing customer interactions and data. This includes processes for collecting, storing, and analyzing customer data, as well as processes for engaging with customers across various touchpoints. By defining and implementing these processes, businesses can ensure that they are able to effectively manage their customer relationships and provide a consistent experience across all touchpoints.

3: Technology

Technology plays a crucial role in CRM. This includes CRM software, which helps businesses manage customer data and interactions. CRM software can track customer interactions, manage customer accounts, and provide insights into customer behavior. In addition to CRM software, other technologies such as analytics tools, marketing automation platforms, and customer service software can also be used to enhance the CRM process. These technologies can help businesses analyze customer data, automate marketing campaigns, and provide better customer service.

In conclusion, the key components of CRM — people, processes, and technology — work together to help businesses manage and improve their relationships with customers. By focusing on these key components, businesses can build stronger relationships with customers, improve customer satisfaction, and drive business growth.

D: CRM vs. Traditional Marketing and Sales

CRM (Customer Relationship Management) and traditional marketing and sales approaches differ in several key ways:

1: Focus on Relationship Building

CRM is centered around building long-term relationships with customers, focusing on understanding their needs and providing personalized experiences. In contrast, traditional marketing and sales often prioritize short-term transactions without necessarily focusing on building lasting relationships.

2: Personalization

CRM emphasizes personalizing interactions with customers based on their preferences, behavior, and past interactions with the business. Traditional marketing and sales approaches tend to be more generic and one-size-fits-all, with less emphasis on tailoring messages and offers to individual customers.

3: Data-Driven Approach

CRM relies heavily on data to understand customers' needs and preferences, track interactions, and measure the effectiveness of marketing campaigns. Traditional marketing and sales approaches may rely more on intuition and experience, without leveraging data to the same extent.

4: Integration of Technology

CRM uses technology, such as CRM software, to manage and analyze customer data and interactions. This allows businesses to streamline processes, improve efficiency, and deliver better customer experiences. In contrast, traditional marketing and sales approaches may rely more on manual processes and may not leverage technology to the same extent.

Overall, CRM represents a shift towards a more customer-centric approach to business, where the focus is on building strong, lasting relationships with customers rather than just making a sale. By leveraging data and technology to personalize interactions and improve customer experiences, businesses can drive customer loyalty and long-term success.

Chapter 2

Building a Customer-Centric Culture

A: Shifting Focus to Customer Needs and Preferences

Building a customer-centric culture is essential for businesses looking to thrive in today's competitive marketplace. This involves shifting the focus from the product or service being sold to the needs and preferences of the customer. Here's a detailed look at how this can be achieved:

1: Understanding Customer Needs and Preferences

The first step in building a customer-centric culture is to understand who your customers are and what they value. This can be achieved through various methods, such as data analysis, surveys, and market research. By gaining insights into customer behavior and preferences, businesses can tailor their products, services, and interactions to better meet the needs of their customers.

2: Proactive Anticipation of Customer Needs

A customer-centric culture goes beyond just reacting to customer inquiries and complaints. It involves proactively anticipating and addressing customer needs before they even arise. This can be achieved by actively seeking feedback from customers, monitoring trends in customer behavior, and staying ahead of competitors in terms of product and service offerings.

3: Personalization of Products and Services

One of the key aspects of a customer-centric culture is the personalization of products and services. This involves tailoring offerings to individual customer preferences and behavior, rather than taking a one-size-fits-all approach. By personalizing products and services, businesses can enhance the customer experience and build stronger relationships with their customers.

4: Empowering Employees to Deliver Exceptional Customer Service

Building a customer-centric culture also involves empowering employees to deliver exceptional customer service. This includes providing employees with the tools, training, and authority they need to make decisions that benefit the customer. By empowering employees, businesses can ensure that customer needs are met quickly and efficiently.

5: Continuous Improvement Based on Customer Feedback

Finally, building a customer-centric culture requires a commitment to continuous improvement based on customer feedback. This means actively seeking feedback from customers, listening to their suggestions and complaints, and using this feedback to improve products, services, and processes.

In conclusion, building a customer-centric culture requires a fundamental shift in focus from the product or service being sold to the needs and preferences of the customer. By understanding customer needs and preferences, proactively anticipating customer needs, personalizing products and services, empowering employees, and continuously improving based on customer feedback, businesses can build strong, lasting relationships with their customers and drive business success.

B: Empowering Employees to Deliver Exceptional Customer Experiences

Empowering employees to deliver exceptional customer experiences is crucial for building a customer-centric culture. Here's a detailed look at how this can be achieved:

1: Authority and Autonomy

Empowering employees involves giving them the authority and autonomy to make decisions that benefit the customer. This means trusting employees to use their judgment and make decisions without needing to seek approval at every step. By giving employees the freedom to act, businesses can respond more quickly to customer needs and provide more personalized service.

2: Resources and Support

Empowering employees also involves providing them with the resources and support they need to deliver exceptional customer experiences. This may include access to training and development opportunities to enhance their skills and knowledge, as well as access to tools and technology that can help them better serve customers. By providing employees with the right resources, businesses can ensure that they are equipped to meet customer needs effectively.

3: Training and Development

Training and development are essential components of empowering employees to deliver exceptional customer experiences. This includes training employees on customer service best practices, as well as providing ongoing development opportunities to enhance their skills and knowledge. By investing in employee training and development, businesses can ensure that their employees are well-equipped to deliver exceptional customer service.

4: Recognition and Rewards

Recognizing and rewarding employees for delivering exceptional customer service is another important aspect of empowering employees. This can include both formal rewards, such as bonuses or incentives, as well as informal recognition, such as praise or commendation. By recognizing and rewarding employees for their efforts, businesses can motivate them to continue delivering exceptional customer service.

5: Encouraging a Customer-Centric Mindset

Finally, building a customer-centric culture involves encouraging a customer-centric mindset among employees. This means helping employees understand the importance of customer satisfaction and loyalty, and how their actions contribute to the overall customer experience. By fostering a customer-centric mindset, businesses can ensure that employees are aligned with the organization's customer-centric goals.

In conclusion, empowering employees to deliver exceptional customer experiences involves giving them the authority, autonomy, and resources they need to succeed. By investing in employee empowerment through training and development, providing them with the right tools and support, and recognizing and rewarding their efforts, businesses can build a customer-centric culture that drives customer satisfaction and loyalty.

C: Implementing Customer Feedback Loops for Continuous Improvement

Implementing customer feedback loops is crucial for building a customer-centric culture. Here's a detailed look at how this can be achieved:

1: Collecting Customer Feedback

The first step in implementing a feedback loop is to collect feedback from customers. This can be done through various channels, such as surveys, reviews, social media, and direct feedback forms. Businesses should use a combination of these channels to gather feedback from a diverse range of customers.

2: Analyzing Feedback

Once feedback has been collected, it should be analyzed to identify key insights and trends. Businesses can use tools such as sentiment analysis and text analytics to help analyze feedback and identify areas for improvement.

3: Acting on Feedback

Perhaps the most important step in the feedback loop is to act on the feedback received. This may involve making changes to products, services, or processes based on customer feedback. It's important to communicate these changes to customers to show that their feedback has been taken seriously.

4: Closing the Loop

Closing the loop involves following up with customers to let them know how their feedback has been used. This can help demonstrate to customers that their feedback is valued and can help build trust and loyalty.

5: Continuous Improvement

Implementing feedback loops is not a one-time process but rather an ongoing commitment to continuous improvement. Businesses should regularly solicit feedback from customers and use this feedback to drive continuous improvement across the organization.

In summary, implementing customer feedback loops is essential for building a customer-centric culture. By collecting, analyzing, and acting on customer feedback, businesses can demonstrate their commitment to customer satisfaction and drive continuous improvement. This can help businesses build stronger relationships with customers, increase customer satisfaction and loyalty, and drive long-term business success.

Chapter 3

Data-Driven CRM Strategies

A: Collecting and Analyzing Customer Data

Collecting and analyzing customer data is a crucial aspect of data-driven CRM strategies. Here's a detailed look at how this process can be carried out:

1: Collecting Customer Data

(i): Surveys and Interviews:

Surveys and interviews can provide valuable insights into customer preferences, opinions, and behavior. They can be conducted online, over the phone, or in person.

(ii): Social Media Monitoring:

Monitoring social media platforms allows businesses to gather information about customer sentiment, interests, and interactions with the brand.

(iii): Website and Mobile App Tracking:

Tracking customer behavior on websites and mobile apps provides data on how customers are interacting with the brand online. This includes pages visited, products viewed, and actions taken.

(iv): Customer Service Interactions:

Customer service interactions, such as calls, emails, and chats, can provide valuable information about customer needs, issues, and preferences.

2: Storing and Organizing Customer Data

(i): Once customer data is collected, it needs to be stored and organized in a way that is accessible and easy to analyze. This is typically done using a CRM system, which can store customer data in a centralized database and organize it based on various criteria, such as customer demographics, purchase history, and interactions.

3: Analyzing Customer Data

(i): Data Analysis Tools:

Data analysis tools can be used to analyze customer data and identify patterns, trends, and insights. These tools can help businesses understand customer behavior, preferences, and needs.

(ii): Personalization:

One of the key benefits of analyzing customer data is the ability to personalize interactions with customers. By understanding customer preferences and behavior, businesses can tailor their products, services, and marketing efforts to better meet the needs of individual customers.

(iii): Improving Customer Experience:

Analyzing customer data can also help businesses identify areas where they can improve the customer experience. For example, if a large number of customers are experiencing issues with a particular product or service, businesses can use this information to make improvements and enhance the overall customer experience.

In conclusion, collecting and analyzing customer data is a foundational aspect of data-driven CRM strategies. By gathering information about customer preferences, behavior, and interactions with the business, businesses can personalize interactions, improve the customer experience, and drive business growth.

B: Leveraging Data for Personalized Marketing and Sales

Leveraging data for personalized marketing and sales is a powerful strategy that can help businesses improve customer engagement and drive sales. Here's how it can be done:

1: Understanding Customer Preferences and Behavior

By collecting and analyzing customer data, businesses can gain insights into customer preferences, behavior, and purchasing history. This information can help businesses understand what motivates customers to make a purchase and tailor their marketing messages and offers accordingly.

2: Personalized Email Marketing

One of the most common ways to leverage customer data for personalized marketing is through email marketing. Businesses can use customer data to segment their email lists based on factors such as past purchase history, demographics, and interests, and send targeted email campaigns that are more likely to resonate with individual customers.

3: Product Recommendations

Another way to leverage customer data for personalized marketing is through product recommendations. By analyzing past purchase history and browsing behavior, businesses can recommend products or services that are relevant to individual customers, increasing the likelihood of a purchase.

4: Customized Offers and Promotions

Businesses can also use customer data to create customized offers and promotions for individual customers. For example, a retail company might offer a discount on a product that a customer has previously shown interest in, or a software company might offer a discount on an upgrade for a product that a customer is currently using.

5: Enhanced Customer Engagement

Personalized marketing and sales efforts are more likely to engage customers and drive them to take action. By delivering messages and offers that are tailored to their interests and preferences, businesses can build stronger relationships with their customers and increase loyalty.

Overall, leveraging data for personalized marketing and sales can help businesses improve customer engagement, drive sales, and build stronger relationships with their customers. By understanding customer preferences and behavior and tailoring their marketing messages and offers accordingly, businesses can create more meaningful and impactful interactions with their customers.

C: Using CRM Software for Data Management and Analysis

Using CRM (Customer Relationship Management) software for data management and analysis is essential for implementing data-driven CRM strategies. Here's a detailed look at how CRM software can be used for these purposes:

1: Centralized Data Storage

CRM software provides a centralized platform for storing customer information in a structured format. This allows businesses to easily access and manage customer data, eliminating the need for disparate systems and manual data entry.

2: Data Analysis Tools

CRM software typically includes tools for analyzing customer data, such as reporting and analytics dashboards.

These tools allow businesses to track key metrics, such as customer acquisition costs, lifetime value, and customer satisfaction, and gain insights into customer behavior and preferences.

3: Personalized Marketing and Sales

CRM software enables businesses to personalize their marketing and sales efforts based on customer data. For example, businesses can use CRM software to segment customers based on demographics, behavior, or purchase history, and tailor their marketing messages and offers accordingly.

4: Automation of Marketing and Sales Processes

CRM software often includes features for automating marketing and sales processes, such as email marketing, lead scoring, and customer segmentation. This can help businesses streamline their CRM efforts, improve efficiency, and drive better results from their customer relationships.

5: Integration with Other Systems

CRM software can be integrated with other systems, such as e-commerce platforms, customer service software, and analytics tools, to provide a more comprehensive view of customer interactions and behavior. This integration allows businesses to make more informed decisions and provide a seamless customer experience across all touchpoints.

In conclusion, CRM software plays a crucial role in data-driven CRM strategies by providing a centralized platform for managing and analyzing customer data. By leveraging

CRM software and adopting a data-driven approach, businesses can build stronger relationships with their customers, increase customer satisfaction, and drive business growth.

Chapter 4

Implementing CRM Systems

A: Choosing the Right CRM System for Your Business

Choosing the right CRM system for your business is a critical decision that can impact your ability to effectively manage customer relationships and drive business growth. Here's a detailed look at how to choose the right CRM system:

1: Assess Your Business Needs and Objectives

The first step in choosing the right CRM system is to assess your business needs and objectives. Consider what features and functionalities are essential for your business, such as contact management, sales automation, customer service, and analytics. Identify your key objectives for implementing a CRM system, such as improving customer satisfaction, increasing sales, or streamlining processes.

2: Research and Compare CRM Systems

Once you have identified your business needs and objectives, research and compare different CRM systems based on your requirements. Look for systems that are user-friendly, scalable, and offer the features you need. Consider factors such as cost, customization options, integration capabilities, and vendor support. There are many CRM systems available in the market, so it's important to do thorough research and compare your options before making a decision.

3: Consider Your Budget

Consider your budget when choosing a CRM system. CRM systems can vary significantly in cost, so it's important to choose a system that fits within your budget while still meeting your business needs. Some CRM systems offer flexible pricing options, such as monthly subscriptions or pay-as-you-go plans, which can be more cost-effective for small businesses or businesses with limited budgets.

4: Evaluate Customization Options

Consider the customization options offered by CRM systems. Choose a system that allows you to customize the software to meet your specific business needs. Look for systems that offer a high degree of flexibility and customization, as this will allow you to tailor the system to your unique requirements.

5: Integration Capabilities

Consider the integration capabilities of the CRM system. Choose a system that integrates seamlessly with your existing systems and software, such as your email marketing platform, e-commerce platform, and customer service software. Integration capabilities are important for ensuring that your CRM system can effectively communicate with other systems and provide a comprehensive view of customer interactions.

6: Vendor Support

Finally, consider the level of support offered by the CRM vendor. Choose a vendor that offers reliable customer support and training to help you get the most out of your CRM system. Look for vendors that offer a range of support options, such as phone support, email support, and online resources, to ensure that you can get help when you need it.

In conclusion, choosing the right CRM system for your business requires careful consideration of your business needs and objectives, as well as thorough research and evaluation of different CRM systems. By following these steps, you can choose a CRM system that meets your business needs and helps you effectively manage customer relationships.

B: Integrating CRM with Existing Systems and Processes

Integrating CRM with existing systems and processes is crucial for maximizing its effectiveness and ensuring seamless operations. Here's a detailed look at how to integrate CRM with existing systems and processes:

1: Identify Systems and Processes to Integrate

The first step in integrating CRM with existing systems and processes is to identify the systems and processes that need to be integrated. This may include email marketing platforms, e-commerce systems, customer service tools, and other business applications.

2: Develop an Integration Plan

Work closely with your CRM vendor to develop an integration plan. This plan should outline the steps involved in integrating CRM with existing systems and processes, including customization of the CRM system to meet integration requirements and data migration strategies to transfer existing data into the CRM system.

3: Customize the CRM System

Depending on your integration requirements, you may need to customize the CRM system to ensure compatibility with existing systems and processes. This may involve modifying the CRM system's configuration, developing custom modules or plugins, or integrating with third-party tools and services.

4: Develop Data Migration Strategies

Data migration is a critical aspect of integrating CRM with existing systems and processes. Develop data migration strategies to transfer existing data into the CRM system, ensuring that data is transferred accurately and securely.

5: Test Integrations

Before fully implementing integrations, it's important to thoroughly test them to ensure that they work as intended and do not disrupt existing operations. Test integrations for compatibility, data accuracy, and performance to identify and address any issues before they impact business operations.

6: Monitor and Maintain Integrations

Once integrations are implemented, monitor them regularly to ensure that they continue to work effectively. Address any issues that arise promptly and make adjustments as needed to optimize performance and compatibility.

In conclusion, integrating CRM with existing systems and processes is essential for maximizing its effectiveness and ensuring seamless operations. By identifying systems and processes to integrate, developing an integration plan, customizing the CRM system, developing data migration strategies, testing integrations, and monitoring and maintaining integrations, businesses can successfully integrate CRM with existing systems and processes to improve efficiency and drive business growth.

C: Training Employees for Effective CRM Adoption

Training employees for effective CRM adoption is crucial for ensuring that your CRM system is used to its full potential. Here's a detailed look at how to train employees for effective CRM adoption:

1: Comprehensive Training

Provide comprehensive training to employees to ensure they understand how to use the CRM system effectively and how it benefits their daily work. Training should cover basic functionalities, such as data entry and management, as well as more advanced features, such as reporting and analytics.

2: Tailored Training for Different Roles

Tailor training programs to different roles within the organization. For example, sales teams may require training on lead management and pipeline tracking, while customer service teams may need training on case management and customer interaction tracking.

3: Hands-On Learning

Provide hands-on learning opportunities to help employees apply what they've learned in training to real-world scenarios. This can include simulations, role-playing exercises, and practical assignments.

4: Ongoing Training and Support

Provide ongoing training and support to help employees continuously improve their CRM skills and knowledge. This can include refresher courses, advanced training sessions, and access to training materials and resources.

5: Create a Culture of CRM Adoption

Encourage employees to embrace the CRM system as a tool to help them better serve customers and achieve their goals. Foster a culture of continuous improvement and innovation, where employees are encouraged to explore new ways of using the CRM system to improve their work.

By providing comprehensive training, tailoring training to different roles, offering hands-on learning opportunities, providing ongoing support, and creating a culture of CRM adoption, businesses can ensure that employees are equipped to effectively use CRM systems and reap the benefits of improved customer relationships, increased efficiency, and business growth.

Chapter 5

CRM in Sales and Marketing

A: Using CRM for Lead Generation and Nurturing

Using CRM for lead generation and nurturing is a strategic approach that helps businesses identify, track, and engage with potential customers throughout the sales process. Here's a detailed look at how CRM can be used for lead generation and nurturing:

1: Lead Identification and Prioritization

CRM systems allow businesses to capture leads from various sources, such as website forms, social media, and events. Leads are then stored in the CRM system, where they can be categorized and prioritized based on criteria such as demographics, behavior, and engagement level.

2: Tracking Interactions with Leads

CRM systems enable businesses to track all interactions with leads, including emails, phone calls, meetings, and website visits. This comprehensive view of lead interactions helps sales teams understand the interests and needs of leads, allowing them to tailor their communication and follow-up strategies accordingly.

3: Personalized Communication

CRM systems enable businesses to personalize their communication with leads based on their interests and behavior. This can include sending targeted emails, offering relevant content, and providing personalized offers. By personalizing communication, businesses can increase engagement and build stronger relationships with leads.

4: Lead Scoring and Qualification

CRM systems can automate lead scoring and qualification processes, allowing businesses to prioritize leads based on their likelihood to convert. This helps sales teams focus their efforts on leads that are most likely to result in a sale, increasing efficiency and effectiveness.

5: Source Tracking and Optimization

CRM systems track the source of leads, such as marketing campaigns or referrals, allowing businesses to measure the effectiveness of their lead generation efforts. This information can be used to optimize marketing strategies and allocate resources more effectively.

6: Automated Lead Nurturing

CRM systems can automate lead nurturing processes, such as sending personalized emails or notifications based on lead behavior and interests. This automated approach helps businesses stay engaged with leads and move them through the sales funnel more efficiently.

In conclusion, using CRM for lead generation and nurturing is a strategic approach that can help businesses identify, track, and engage with potential customers more effectively. By leveraging CRM systems for lead generation and nurturing, businesses can increase their sales effectiveness, improve customer relationships, and drive business growth.

B: Tracking Customer Interactions and Engagement

Tracking customer interactions and engagement is a key function of CRM systems, providing businesses with valuable insights into customer behavior and preferences. Here's a detailed look at how CRM systems track customer interactions and engagement:

1: Centralized Customer Data

CRM systems centralize customer data, including interactions and engagement across various touchpoints. This allows businesses to have a complete view of each customer's history, preferences, and behavior, enabling them to provide personalized and targeted communication.

2: Multi-Channel Interaction Tracking

CRM systems track customer interactions across multiple channels, such as email, phone calls, social media, and website visits. This comprehensive view of interactions helps businesses understand how customers are engaging with their brand and allows them to tailor their communication strategies accordingly.

3: Personalized Communication

By tracking customer interactions, CRM systems enable businesses to personalize their communication with customers. For example, businesses can send targeted emails based on past interactions or offer personalized recommendations based on customer preferences.

4: Customer Engagement Metrics

CRM systems track customer engagement metrics, such as email open rates, click-through rates, and social media interactions. These metrics provide valuable insights into how customers are engaging with the brand and can help businesses measure the effectiveness of their marketing campaigns and content.

5: Automated Engagement Tracking

CRM systems can automate the tracking of customer interactions and engagement, reducing the manual effort required to capture and analyze this data. This automation allows businesses to track interactions in real time and respond quickly to customer inquiries and feedback.

6: Improved Customer Service

By tracking customer interactions and engagement, CRM systems help businesses provide better customer service. For example, businesses can use CRM data to anticipate customer needs, resolve issues more efficiently, and provide personalized support.

In conclusion, CRM systems play a crucial role in tracking customer interactions and engagement across various touchpoints. By centralizing customer data and providing insights into customer behavior, CRM systems help businesses personalize their communication, improve customer service, and drive customer loyalty.

C: Measuring ROI of CRM Strategies

Measuring the Return on Investment (ROI) of CRM strategies is crucial for evaluating their effectiveness and optimizing future efforts. Here's a detailed look at how to measure the ROI of CRM strategies:

1: Define Key Performance Indicators (KPIs)

Start by defining the KPIs that will be used to measure the ROI of CRM strategies. These KPIs should be aligned with your business goals and objectives. Common KPIs for measuring CRM ROI include:

(i): Conversion Rate: The percentage of leads that result in a sale.

(ii): Customer Acquisition Cost (CAC): The cost associated with acquiring a new customer.

(iii): Customer Lifetime Value (CLTV): The total revenue a customer is expected to generate over their lifetime.

(iv): Customer Retention Rate: The percentage of customers that continue to do business with the company over time.

2: Track and Analyze CRM Data:

Use your CRM system to track and analyze data related to your KPIs. This includes tracking customer interactions, sales performance, and marketing campaigns. By analyzing this data, you can gain insights into the effectiveness of your CRM strategies and identify areas for improvement.

3: Calculate ROI:

Once you have tracked and analyzed your CRM data, you can calculate the ROI of your CRM strategies. The formula for calculating ROI is:

$$ROI = \left(\frac{\text{Net Profit} - \text{Cost of CRM Strategy}}{\text{Cost of CRM Strategy}}\right) \times 100\%$$

Where:

(i): Net Profit is the total revenue generated from CRM strategies minus the total cost of implementing those strategies.

(ii): Cost of CRM Strategy includes the cost of CRM software, implementation, training, and any other related expenses.

4: Evaluate Results and Make Improvements

Based on the ROI analysis, evaluate the effectiveness of your CRM strategies and identify areas for improvement.

This could involve adjusting your CRM strategy, investing in additional training, or implementing new CRM features to drive better results.

5: Continuously Monitor and Improve

Measuring the ROI of CRM strategies is an ongoing process. Continuously monitor your KPIs and adjust your CRM strategies as needed to improve ROI over time.

In conclusion, measuring the ROI of CRM strategies is essential for evaluating their effectiveness and optimizing future efforts. By defining KPIs, tracking and analyzing CRM data, calculating ROI, evaluating results, and continuously monitoring and improving, businesses can ensure that their CRM strategies are driving tangible results and contributing to business growth.

Chapter 6

CRM in Customer Service

A: Improving Customer Support with CRM

Improving customer support with CRM involves leveraging customer data and automation to enhance the overall customer experience. Here's a detailed look at how CRM can improve customer support:

1: Centralized Customer Information

CRM systems provide a centralized platform for storing and managing customer information, including contact details, purchase history, and previous interactions. This allows customer support agents to access relevant customer information quickly, enabling them to provide personalized support.

2: Personalized Support

With access to customer information, support agents can provide personalized support tailored to each customer's needs. This can include addressing customers by name, referencing previous interactions, and offering relevant solutions based on customer history.

3: Automation of Support Processes

CRM systems can automate certain aspects of customer support, such as ticket routing and response. Automated processes can help reduce response times and improve overall efficiency, allowing support agents to focus on more complex issues that require human intervention.

4: Improved Communication

CRM systems enable seamless communication between support agents and customers across multiple channels, such as email, phone, and chat. This helps ensure that customers receive timely and consistent support regardless of the channel they use to contact the business.

5: Tracking Support Metrics

CRM systems can track key support metrics, such as response times, resolution rates, and customer satisfaction scores. By analyzing these metrics, businesses can identify trends and areas for improvement in their support processes.

6: Integration with Other Systems

CRM systems can be integrated with other systems, such as ticketing systems and knowledge bases, to provide a more comprehensive support experience. Integration allows support agents to access relevant information and tools directly from the CRM system, streamlining the support process.

In conclusion, CRM plays a crucial role in improving customer support by providing a centralized platform for managing customer information, automating support processes, and tracking support metrics. By leveraging CRM effectively, businesses can enhance the overall customer experience and build stronger relationships with their customers.

B: Handling Customer Complaints and Feedback

Handling customer complaints and feedback effectively is crucial for maintaining customer satisfaction and loyalty. Here's a detailed look at how CRM can help in this regard:

1: Structured Process

CRM systems provide a structured process for logging, tracking, and resolving customer complaints. This helps ensure that complaints are addressed promptly and efficiently, leading to improved customer satisfaction.

2: Categorization and Prioritization

CRM systems can categorize and prioritize complaints based on factors such as severity and impact. This helps businesses identify critical issues that require immediate attention and allocate resources accordingly.

3: Automation of Feedback Handling

CRM systems can automate the handling of customer feedback, such as surveys and reviews. This automation streamlines the feedback collection process and allows businesses to gather valuable insights into customer satisfaction and sentiment.

4: Analysis of Feedback

CRM systems can analyze customer feedback to identify trends and patterns. By analyzing feedback, businesses can gain valuable insights into areas for improvement and take corrective actions to enhance customer satisfaction.

5: Integration with Other Systems

CRM systems can be integrated with other systems, such as customer service software and ticketing systems, to provide a more comprehensive view of customer complaints and feedback. Integration allows businesses to track complaints and feedback across multiple channels and ensure a consistent response.

6: Continuous Improvement

By leveraging CRM systems to handle customer complaints and feedback, businesses can continuously improve their products, services, and processes. This iterative approach to improvement helps businesses stay responsive to customer needs and maintain high levels of customer satisfaction.

In conclusion, CRM systems play a crucial role in handling customer complaints and feedback by providing a structured process, categorizing and prioritizing complaints, automating feedback handling, analyzing feedback, integrating with other systems, and enabling continuous improvement. By leveraging CRM effectively, businesses can enhance customer satisfaction, loyalty, and retention.

C: Building Customer Loyalty through Exceptional Service

Building customer loyalty through exceptional service is a key goal for businesses, and CRM systems play a crucial role in achieving this. Here's a detailed look at how CRM can help build customer loyalty:

1: Personalized Service

CRM systems enable businesses to provide personalized service by storing customer information, such as purchase history, preferences, and interactions. This allows businesses to tailor their interactions with customers, making them feel valued and appreciated.

2: Efficient Support

CRM systems help businesses provide efficient support by streamlining customer service processes. With CRM, customer service agents can access relevant customer information quickly, enabling them to resolve issues faster and more effectively.

3: Proactive Engagement

CRM systems enable businesses to engage with customers proactively. For example, businesses can use CRM to send personalized offers or recommendations based on customer preferences, increasing customer engagement and loyalty.

4: Upselling and Cross-Selling

CRM systems can help businesses identify opportunities to upsell or cross-sell to existing customers. By analyzing customer data, businesses can offer relevant products or services, increasing customer loyalty and lifetime value.

5: Loyalty Programs

CRM systems can help businesses manage loyalty programs by tracking customer participation and rewards. By offering incentives for repeat purchases, businesses can encourage customer loyalty and retention.

6: Feedback and Improvement

CRM systems enable businesses to gather feedback from customers and use it to improve their products, services, and processes. By listening to customer feedback, businesses can demonstrate their commitment to customer satisfaction and loyalty.

In conclusion, CRM systems are essential for building customer loyalty through exceptional service. By providing personalized service, efficient support, proactive engagement, upselling and cross-selling opportunities, loyalty programs, and feedback mechanisms, businesses can enhance the overall customer experience and drive customer satisfaction and loyalty.

Chapter 7

CRM Best Practices

A: Building Long-Term Relationships vs. Short-Term Transactions

Building long-term relationships with customers is essential for businesses looking to create a loyal customer base and sustainable growth. Here's a detailed look at how to build long-term relationships vs. short-term transactions using CRM:

1: Understanding Customer Needs

CRM systems enable businesses to gather and analyze customer data, helping them understand their customers' needs and preferences. By understanding what motivates their customers, businesses can tailor their products, services, and marketing efforts to meet those needs.

2: Personalized Engagement

CRM systems allow businesses to engage with customers in a personalized way. This can include sending personalized messages, offering tailored promotions, and providing customized support. By personalizing their interactions, businesses can show customers that they are valued and appreciated.

3: Consistent Communication

CRM systems help businesses maintain consistent communication with their customers. This can include regular updates, newsletters, and special offers. By staying in touch with customers, businesses can build trust and loyalty over time.

4: Anticipating Needs

CRM systems can help businesses anticipate their customers' needs. By analyzing past purchase behavior and interactions, businesses can predict what their customers might need in the future and proactively offer solutions.

5: Providing Value

Building long-term relationships requires businesses to provide ongoing value to their customers. This can include offering educational content, exclusive offers, and personalized recommendations. By providing value, businesses can keep customers engaged and loyal.

6: Resolving Issues Promptly

CRM systems can help businesses resolve customer issues promptly and efficiently. By addressing customer concerns quickly, businesses can demonstrate their commitment to customer satisfaction and build trust.

7: Seeking Feedback

CRM systems enable businesses to gather feedback from customers. By seeking feedback, businesses can show customers that their opinions are valued and use that feedback to improve their products and services.

In conclusion, building long-term relationships with customers requires businesses to understand their needs, engage with them in a personalized way, maintain consistent communication, anticipate their needs, provide ongoing value, resolve issues promptly, and seek feedback. By focusing on building long-term relationships, businesses can create a loyal customer base and drive sustainable growth.

B: Personalizing Customer Interactions for Maximum Impact

Personalizing customer interactions is crucial for businesses aiming to create meaningful connections with their customers. Here's a detailed look at how to personalize customer interactions for maximum impact using CRM:

1: Collecting Customer Data

CRM systems allow businesses to collect and store customer data, including demographics, purchase history, preferences, and interactions. This data serves as the foundation for personalization efforts.

2: Analyzing Customer Data

CRM systems help businesses analyze customer data to gain insights into customer behavior and preferences. By analyzing this data, businesses can identify patterns and trends that can be used to personalize interactions.

3: Segmentation

CRM systems enable businesses to segment their customer base based on various criteria, such as demographics, purchase history, and behavior. Segmentation allows businesses to tailor their communications and offers to specific customer segments, increasing their relevance and impact.

4: Personalized Communication

CRM systems enable businesses to send personalized communications to customers, such as personalized emails, messages, and offers. Personalized communication makes customers feel valued and understood, leading to increased engagement and loyalty.

5: Product Recommendations

CRM systems can analyze customer data to provide personalized product recommendations. By recommending products that align with customers' preferences and past purchases, businesses can increase the likelihood of a purchase and enhance the overall customer experience.

6: Targeted Marketing Campaigns

CRM systems allow businesses to create targeted marketing campaigns based on customer segments and preferences. By targeting the right audience with relevant offers, businesses can improve campaign effectiveness and drive higher ROI.

7: Feedback and Iteration

CRM systems enable businesses to gather feedback from customers on personalized interactions. This feedback can be used to refine and improve personalization efforts over time, ensuring that interactions remain relevant and impactful.

In conclusion, personalizing customer interactions is essential for businesses looking to create meaningful connections with their customers. By leveraging CRM systems to collect, analyze, and leverage customer data effectively, businesses can personalize interactions and create more engaging and impactful experiences for their customers.

C: Balancing Automation with Human Touch

Balancing automation with a human touch is crucial in customer relationship management (CRM) to ensure that interactions remain personalized and empathetic. Here's a detailed look at how to achieve this balance:

1: Understanding Customer Needs

Businesses should use automation to gather data and understand customer needs, but also ensure that human interaction is available for more complex queries or issues.

2: Using Automation for Routine Tasks

Automation can be used for tasks such as data entry, lead scoring, and scheduling appointments, freeing up human agents to focus on more value-added activities.

3: Providing Personalized Interactions

CRM systems can be used to personalize interactions based on customer data, such as purchase history and preferences. Automated messages and offers can be tailored to individual customers to make them feel valued.

4: Engaging with Customers Directly

While automation can handle many customer interactions, businesses should be prepared to engage with customers directly when necessary. This includes responding to individual inquiries and providing personalized assistance.

5: Monitoring and Adjusting

It's important to continuously monitor the balance between automation and human touch and adjust strategies as needed. This can help ensure that interactions remain relevant and effective.

6: Training and Empowering Employees

Providing training and resources to employees can help them feel confident in engaging with customers directly.

Empowered employees are more likely to provide personalized and empathetic service.

7: Soliciting Feedback

Businesses should solicit feedback from customers to ensure that automated interactions are meeting their needs. This feedback can help identify areas for improvement and guide future interactions.

In conclusion, balancing automation with a human touch in CRM is essential for providing personalized and empathetic customer experiences. By understanding customer needs, using automation for routine tasks, providing personalized interactions, engaging with customers directly, monitoring and adjusting strategies, training and empowering employees, and soliciting feedback, businesses can create a customer-centric approach that drives satisfaction and loyalty.

Chapter 8
Future Trends in CRM

A: AI and Machine Learning in CRM

AI and Machine Learning (ML) are revolutionizing Customer Relationship Management (CRM) by enabling businesses to analyze data more effectively and personalize interactions with customers. Here's a detailed look at how AI and ML are transforming CRM:

1: Predictive Lead Scoring

AI and ML algorithms can analyze customer data to predict which leads are most likely to convert into customers. This helps businesses prioritize leads and focus their efforts on those with the highest potential, improving sales effectiveness.

2: Chatbots for Customer Service

AI-powered chatbots can provide instant, 24/7 customer support by answering common questions and resolving issues. Chatbots can also escalate more complex inquiries to human agents, improving response times and customer satisfaction.

3: Personalized Marketing Campaigns

AI and ML can analyze customer behavior and preferences to create personalized marketing campaigns. By delivering targeted messages and offers, businesses can increase engagement and conversion rates.

4: Customer Insights and Analytics

AI and ML algorithms can analyze customer data to uncover valuable insights and trends. This information can help businesses understand their customers better and make data-driven decisions to improve products, services, and marketing strategies.

5: Automation of Routine Tasks

AI can automate routine tasks, such as data entry and scheduling, freeing up employees to focus on more strategic activities. This can improve efficiency and productivity across the organization.

6: Improved Customer Engagement

AI-powered tools can analyze customer interactions across multiple channels, such as email, social media, and website, to provide a more holistic view of the customer journey. This enables businesses to engage with customers more effectively and provide a seamless experience across channels.

7: Enhanced Customer Service

AI can analyze customer inquiries and provide relevant information or solutions in real-time. This can help businesses resolve customer issues faster and improve overall customer satisfaction.

In conclusion, AI and ML are transforming CRM by enabling businesses to analyze data more effectively, personalize interactions with customers, and improve overall customer experience. By leveraging these technologies, businesses can stay ahead of the competition and drive business growth.

B: Omni-Channel Customer Engagement

Omni-channel customer engagement is a crucial aspect of modern CRM, focusing on providing a seamless and consistent customer experience across all channels. Here's a detailed look at how omni-channel customer engagement is transforming CRM:

1: Integrated Customer Experience

Omni-channel CRM integrates customer interactions and data from all channels, including social media, mobile apps, websites, and physical stores. This allows businesses to provide a unified and consistent experience regardless of the channel customers use.

2: Personalized Interactions

By integrating customer data from multiple channels, businesses can gain a holistic view of each customer's preferences, behaviors, and interactions. This enables them to personalize interactions and offers based on individual customer preferences, leading to higher engagement and customer satisfaction.

3: Improved Customer Service

Omni-channel CRM enables businesses to provide better customer service by allowing customers to contact them through their preferred channels. Whether customers prefer to communicate via email, phone, chat, or social media, businesses can provide a consistent level of service across all channels.

4: Seamless Customer Journey

With omni-channel CRM, businesses can create a seamless customer journey that spans multiple channels. For example, a customer might research a product on a website, view reviews on social media, and make a purchase through a mobile app, all while receiving personalized recommendations and support along the way.

5: Enhanced Customer Insights

By tracking customer interactions across multiple channels, businesses can gain valuable insights into customer behavior and preferences. This data can be used to improve marketing strategies, product offerings, and customer service initiatives.

6: Increased Customer Loyalty

Providing a seamless and consistent experience across all channels can help businesses build customer loyalty. Customers who have positive experiences are more likely to become repeat customers and advocates for the brand.

In conclusion, omni-channel customer engagement is transforming CRM by providing a seamless and consistent experience across all channels. By integrating customer interactions and data from multiple channels, businesses can personalize interactions, improve customer service, and increase customer loyalty.

C: Ethical Considerations in CRM

Ethical considerations in CRM are critical as businesses collect, store, and use customer data. Here's a detailed look at the key ethical considerations in CRM:

1: Data Security

Businesses must ensure that customer data is stored securely and protected from unauthorized access, breaches, and cyber attacks. This includes implementing strong security measures such as encryption, access controls, and regular security audits.

2: Consent Management

Businesses should obtain explicit consent from customers before collecting, storing, or using their personal data. This includes providing clear and transparent information about how their data will be used and giving customers the option to opt out or withdraw consent at any time.

3: Privacy Protection

Businesses should respect customer privacy by only collecting and using data that is necessary for the intended purpose. They should also ensure that customer data is anonymized or pseudonymized where possible to protect privacy.

4: Transparency and Accountability

Businesses should be transparent about their data practices and accountable for how they use customer data. This includes providing clear privacy policies, data retention policies, and procedures for handling data breaches.

5: Avoiding Algorithmic Bias

Businesses should ensure that their algorithms are free from bias and discrimination. This includes regularly auditing algorithms for bias and taking steps to mitigate any bias that is identified.

6: Compliance with Regulations

Businesses must comply with relevant regulations, such as the General Data Protection Regulation (GDPR) and the California Consumer Privacy Act (CCPA). This includes obtaining explicit consent from customers, providing access to their data, and allowing them to request deletion of their data.

7: Data Minimization

Businesses should only collect and retain customer data that is necessary for the intended purpose. This helps minimize the risk of data breaches and ensures that customer data is not used inappropriately.

By addressing these ethical considerations, businesses can build trust with their customers and enhance the overall customer experience. Ethical CRM practices can also help businesses avoid costly fines and reputational damage associated with data breaches and privacy violations.

In conclusion

Customer Relationship Management (CRM) is not merely a business strategy but a philosophy that places the customer at the core of all business activities. By adopting a customer-centric approach and implementing the principles and best practices outlined in this book, businesses can cultivate meaningful and lasting relationships with their customers, leading to increased loyalty, satisfaction, and ultimately, business success.

CRM emphasizes the importance of understanding customer needs and preferences, engaging with customers in a personalized manner, and providing exceptional customer service. By doing so, businesses can build trust with their customers and differentiate themselves from competitors.

Furthermore, CRM involves collecting and analyzing customer data to gain insights into customer behavior and preferences. This data-driven approach enables businesses to tailor their products, services, and marketing efforts to better meet the needs of their customers, leading to higher levels of customer satisfaction and loyalty.

Overall, CRM is a powerful strategy that can help businesses build strong, long-term relationships with their customers, drive business growth, and achieve sustainable competitive advantage. By embracing CRM as a philosophy and implementing its principles and best practices, businesses can position themselves for success in today's competitive marketplace.

www.ingramcontent.com/pod-product-compliance
Lightning Source LLC
Chambersburg PA
CBHW070412230526
45471CB00006B/2773